Difficult Riddles For Kids

300 Difficult Riddles and Brain Teasers

to Challenge Kids and Families

Riddle Books For Kids Vol 1

Smile Zone

ISBN: 9781689569972

Table of Contents

Introduction

So you are someone who enjoys a good riddle? Riddles are fun for both the asker, the asked, and anyone else who is present for this playful battle of wits. The best thing about riddles, though? They can help you have fun just about anywhere. From a sunny day at the park to a rainy, cup of cocoa type of day, to those seemingly never-ending car rides, this book can keep any riddle fan satisfied, and perplexed, for hours.

What follows are the hardest riddles and most challenging brainteasers we could come up with. Each chapter is sorted by difficulty from 1 to 5. A 1-star riddle will be simple, though there is no shame if you have a hard time with it, it is a riddle after all. Then we go all the way up to 5-star riddle. These are the toughest of the tough. Meant to challenge your logic, reasoning skills, and creative thinking. Additionally, we have a chapter of brain teaser questions. While not riddles, they are also meant to challenge how you think about questions and their answers. You might need a pencil and paper for that chapter. Finally, as a bonus, we included a special chapter of 6-star riddles at the end of the book. These 6-star riddles are beyond difficult and some of the most complex riddles we have ever had the pleasure of thinking about. Looking for a real challenge, then those are the riddles for you.

One last note from the author: If you feel stumped, don't worry. A riddle is supposed to stump you. That is what it is supposed to do. Looking at the answer isn't against the rules, it is just what you do at the end of a tough riddle. And in the end, right or wrong, the important part is to enjoy yourself. And if you need to look to know the answer, that's okay. It will make you a stronger riddler in the future. So remember, think long, think hard, think creatively, and have fun.

And now for our very first riddle:

"In a riddle whose answer is chess, what is the only prohibited word?"

-Jorge Luis Borges

Navigation Tip

All the answers will be in the back of the book.

Chapter One

One Star Riddle

1. One Star Riddle #1

The one who crafts it, always sells it

The one who buys it is never the one who uses it

The one that uses it will never know they are.

What is it?

2. One Star Riddle #2

I build up castles

I tear down mountains

I make some men blind, while others I see clearly

What am I?

3. One Star Riddle #3

Whoever forges it, tells it not

Whoever takes it, knows it not

Whoever spots it, wants it not

What is it?

4. One Star Riddle #4

I can be liquid or solid, or all around the air

You find me in every home in bottle, bucket, or square

What am I?

5. One Star Riddle #5

As I walking to the town of Finster

I met a woman with seven misters

Each mister had seven boxes

Each box had seven foxes

Each fox had seven kits

Kits, foxes, boxes, and misters

How many were there going to Finster?

6. One Star Riddle #6

To me, the world occupies little space

To you, I am always changing place

No food I eat, but, by my power

Create what millions will devour

7. One Star Riddle #7

Fly all day long, but don't go anywhere

I am standard but I am different everywhere you go

8. One Star Riddle #8

Call to me and I disappear

Ignore me and I stay

I am truly rare at any time.

But you are more likely to find me at night than day

9. One Star Riddle #9

What has cities, but no houses; forests, but no trees; and water, but no fish?

10. One Star Riddle #10

A man runs away from home. He turns left, and keeps desperately running. After sometime he turns left again and keeps running at a rapid pace. He later turns left once more and runs back home.

Who was the man in the mask that so concerned him?

11. One Star Riddle #11

You get many of me, but never enough

After the last one, your life is promised to snuff

You may have me but one day a year

But it is the day that for you everyone will cheer

12. One Star Riddle #12

What is the only situation you will want to go on red and stop when you get to green?

13. One Star Riddle #13

When I'm born I fly. When I'm alive I lay. When I'm dead I run

14. One Star Riddle #14

I have six faces but cannot wear a mask

21 eyes but cannot see

What am I?

15. One Star Riddle #15

Shifting, Shifting, Drifting deep

Underneath, great and mighty cities sleep

Swirling, swirling, All around

I'm only where no water is found

16. One Star Riddle #16

My thunder comes before my lightning

My lightning comes before my rain

And my rain brings new earth and burns all around it

What am I?

17. One Star Riddle #17

We are five little friends and common word cohorts

You will find us all inside a tennis court

18. One Star Riddle #18

I always bring you up, never down

I always turn left, never right

I am always moving, even when I'm frozen

19. One Star Riddle #19

The answer I give is yes, but what I mean is no. There is no intent to confuse or

And I am being 100% honest. What was the question?

20. One Star Riddle #20

I am irresistible

For all needs seem met with me

I will easily bend to your will

But you will have to work hard to free me

21. One Star Riddle #21

A cloud is my mother

The wind is my father

My son is the swift running stream

A rainbow is my end

Until I am born again

I will make the earth gleam

22. One Star Riddle #22

I can be written, spoken, and seen. Though most prefer me live at the scene.

23. One Star Riddle #23

Sometimes I shine, sometimes I'm dull

If my size matters is something you'll mull

I can be pointy and I can be curved

What matters most is the purpose I serve

I can split and I can pierce

I am a tool most fierce

What am I?

24. One Star Riddle #24

I flicker and glow

I tell stories and put on a show

To create me you must first trick the eye

In to seeing one image where many lie

What am I?

25. One Star Riddle #25

People say I was sown by a folk hero

You seem me in bushel, barrel, and bob

I can be both food and drink

And I can put doctors out of a job

What am I?

26. One Star Riddle #26

I can easily bring you down if you aren't careful

But I can be just as easily be crushed by you

I like to split deserts a lot

But I'm very healthy too

What am I?

27. One Star Riddle #27

I enrage bulls when they see me

But I make you stop completely

And if you see me run from you

You should get to a doctor immediately

28. One Star Riddle #28

Thirty men and only two women, but the women hold sway over all

Dressed in black and white, the battle lines drawn

It is on a board that they show their brawn

You are their lord

But to only one color you are sworn

29. One Star Riddle #29

Something different to show every week

But I'm still in the same place

If you're eating from my buckets

Then it's probably butter that you taste

30. One Star Riddle #30

I cannot hear or even see

But sense light and sounds near me

Sometimes, innocent, I end up on the hook

Or might even spot me deep within a book

31. One Star Riddle #31

If you lose one of me, you are bewildered, looking everywhere

If you lose two of me, you are blissfully unaware

You'll have a reminder, all things told

Especially when you are forced to walk in the cold

32. One Star Riddle #32

A king, queen, and two twins all lay in a large room

They lie on their backs, and are covered in sheets

They did not die as a family, nay they were never alive to begin with

What are they?

33. One Star Riddle #33

Though I live and work beneath a roof

You will never allow me to dry

If you will only hold me and still me

I swear I will not lie

34. One Star Riddle #34

It can take me a while to get dirty but it takes about half an hour to clean me

It takes years for me to be tall but I can be short in but a moment

And while shortening me might take a weight off your shoulders

It can be a big decision

What am I?

35. One Star Riddle #35

I am roomy inside but still very small

I am part of the hand, but have no life in me at all

36. One Star Riddle #36

What goes all around and around the wood, but never goes into the wood?

37. One Star Riddle #37

Rita died in Florida

Shortly after, Trisha died at sea

Nobody mourned

In fact, everyone was as happy as can be

Why?

38. One Star Riddle #38

I fly straight and true

My feathers don't propel me, but give me direction

I can feed my maker

I am usually one of a collection

39. One Star Riddle #39

What has thirteen hearts but no muscle, soul, or blood?

40. One Star Riddle #40

What flares up and does a lot of good, and when it dies it is not even worth its wood

41. One Star Riddle #41

Never alive to begin with but now practically extinct

How we miss the rattle of letters pressing that ribbon of ink

What is it?

Chapter Two

Two Stars Riddle

1. Two Stars Riddle #1

What always runs but never walks

Has a mouth but never talks

Has a bed but never sleeps

Has a head but never weeps?

2. Two Stars Riddle #2

I weigh less than what makes me

I keep the rest of my body hidden from thee

What am I?

3. Two Stars Riddle #3

You never see me blink

But often see me staring

Upon your fashion choices

My opinion holds much bearing

What am I?

4. Two Stars Riddle #4

I can be short, or I can be long

I can be grown, and I can be bought for a song

I can be decorated, or left bare

I can be round, or I can be square

What am I?

home in bottle, bucket, or square

What am I?

5. Two Stars Riddle #5

The more you take, the more you leave behind

The rougher you take them, the more noticeable it is?

6. Two Stars Riddle #6

When you need me

You toss me away

But when you're done with me

You end up yanking me back

7. Two Stars Riddle #7

I am bought for eating, but nobody ever eats me

Knives are applied to me, but I am never cut

I am covered in delicious sauces, but it would be considered rude to taste me

8. Two Stars Riddle #8

I cannot walk but you might catch me running

Wherever I go, thoughts follows me close behind, though I pay them little mind

9. Two Stars Riddle #9

I don't have eyes, but did once see

Before I had thoughts, but now I'm hollow and empty

10. Two Stars Riddle #10

I have keys, but no locks and space, and no rooms

You can enter, but you can't go outside

What am I?

11. Two Stars Riddle #11

What hole do you mend with holes

Often kept on pulley and poles

Can be used to gather en mass

Or to trap those who trespass

12. Two Stars Riddle #12

I have one eye

But what I keep buried deep inside

Is more likely to make you cry

Than I

What am I?

13. Two Stars Riddle #13

Look into my face and I'm everyone. I will never close my eyes when you can see me

What am I?

14. Two Stars Riddle #14

What relies on columns but isn't a house

And struggles for truth but can never speak for itself?

15. Two Stars Riddle #15

I am truly nothing at all, Yet I am easily found

Ignore me, and you will end up wearing a crown!

16. Two Stars Riddle #16

What has four wings but cannot fly

And uses the wind to make something you will buy?

17. Two Stars Riddle #17

I'm an old relative who's hands can't hold anything

But whose voice can garner the attention of all

What am I?

18. Two Stars Riddle #18

I am a mother from a family of eight

Spins around all day despite my size

Had a ninth sibling before finding out its fake

Had to be re-categorized

What am I?

19. Two Stars Riddle #19

The stack is sent far and wide

Full of what's new

But by tomorrow no one will buy it

20. Two Stars Riddle #20

My step is slow, the snow's my breath

I give the ground a grinding breadth

My marching will be the end of me

Slain by sun or lost out at sea

21. Two Stars Riddle #21

Two legs have I, and this will confound

Only when I rest do they touch the ground

What am I?

22. Two Stars Riddle #22

What goes up, but at the same time goes down?

The faster to the sky, the harder toward the ground

Its present tense and past tense too

Come for a ride, just me and you!

23. Two Stars Riddle #23

The name I'm given is never mine

No one considers my weight while in their prime

Once you pick yours it won't be long

Before your special mourning dawns

24. Two Stars Riddle #24

Glistening points

Downward they thrust

Sparkling spears

That can never rust

25. Two Stars Riddle #25

I bring together a split of land

I can be built hand in hand

I am the thing for which poor swimmers yearn

I am the thing that poor friends will burn

26. Two Stars Riddle #26

As I went across the bridge, I met a man with a load of wood which was neither straight nor crooked. He carried it neither by box or beast but instead by hand, in a bag lest it sift like sand. What kind of wood was it?

27. Two Stars Riddle #27

I may seem flat but I'm not shallow

I have hidden depths you can't fathom

I have much to offer

But I take as much as I please

But that is the danger with things as beautiful as I

I can be as calm or as wrathful as anyone

Yet I have no heart at all

No man can own me, though many have tried

And everyone who has ever thought to tame me has died.

28. Two Stars Riddle #28

You can collect me, toss me, and spin me

Move me just right and you can make decisions with me

People all around the world have different names for me

What am I?

29. Two Stars Riddle #29

Many hear me after they cry

And where I exist I multiply

Hard to track unless your hearing is keen

And I am only ever heard and never ever seen

What am I?

30. Two Stars Riddle #30

I had a bright start

but I caved to the pressure

It is hard to feel happy and sunny

When everything collapses around you

What am I?

31. Two Stars Riddle #31

I have no wallet but I travel without loan

Where I ride, only a sheet fits inside

But that doesn't mean I travel alone

32. Two Stars Riddle #32

I have memories, but are given, not my own

Whatever is on my inside is what is shown

If I'm ever different it's because you changed me

If your especially proud you'll hang me

33. Two Stars Riddle #33

I drape the hills in a blanket of white

I do not swallow, but fingers I bite

Many try and break me but I'm a tough nut to crack

If you think me unpredictable then you don't know jack

34. Two Stars Riddle #34

I open to close but I close to open

I'm surrounded by water but I'm never soaking

I was used to keep enemies at bay

But now I control traffic day to day

35. Two Stars Riddle #35

How many letters are in the answer to this riddle?

36. Two Stars Riddle #36

What demands an answer, but asks no questions?

Helps you remember distant relations?

Can never be used for free, unless it is an emergency?

37. Two Stars Riddle #37

Sometimes I'm high and sometimes low

This is easy to see based on where the lines go

My orders come from the sky

I make the planks beneath fall and rise

38. Two Stars Riddle #38

There are several different kinds

But the one you pick doesn't do its job

But if you crack someone else's

Then you just finished a job of your own

39. Two Stars Riddle #39

Tall as can be, dressed in white

my bridal veil is shiny and bright

Up all night, I can never sleep

If I ever rest, many will weep

Upon the shores since my days are long and lonely

My sole guardian is my one and only

What am I?

40. Two Stars Riddle #40

I love to dance all around

But high above the boring ground

I'm quite strung out when way up high

I like to sail, but prefer to stay dry

I need air, but do not breathe

A helpful hand is all I need

What am I?

41. Two Stars Riddle #41

You eat something neither plant nor animal

It is the son of the sea

But if water touches it, it dies

42. Two Stars Riddle #42

Big as a mountain

Small as a pea by comparison

Endlessly swimming in a water-less sea

Without rhyme or reason

43. Two Stars Riddle #43

It is destruction composed out of thin air

You hear it roar and run for the cellar

Through barns and houses it will tear

It is a mystery what it will ruin and what it will spare

Chapter Three

Three Stars Riddle

1. Three Stars Riddle #1

I give you a group of three preparing a meal.

One is squat and heavy, with no inclination to rise.

The second eats as much as is given to him, and if you ever stop he dies.

The third is flighty and ambitious, always on the rise.

Who are they?

2. Three Stars Riddle #2

Only one color, but never one size

Stuck at the bottom, yet I stretch to the sky

Come out in the sun, but avoid the rain

Doing as you do with none of the gain

What Am I?

3. Three Stars Riddle #3

One by one we fall from our lofty home, down into the depths of past

And our world is ever a-tumble in a wish that time weren't as fast

What are we?

4. Three Stars Riddle #4

Kings and queens can cling to power and the jester's has his call

But destiny may play its hand and the common one can outrank them all

What is it?

5. Three Stars Riddle #5

Alive without air

Has never taken a breath

Always fearful of the snare

And as cold as death

Clad in mail never clinking

Never thirsty, ever drinking

6. Three Stars Riddle #6

All day I go in circles

But ever straight ahead

If I ever complain, it's only a squeak

No matter where I am led

7. Three Stars Riddle #7

Poke your fingers in my eyes

And I will open my jaws wide

Linen or paper, taught or loll

I will devour them all.

8. Three Stars Riddle #8

I fly to any foreign parts

Pulled along by the unfurled

My mind relies on maps and charts

To bring me all over the world

My main task is to do exactly what I am

But I can also bring eager people from land to different land

9. Three Stars Riddle #9

Flat as can be, round as a ring; Has eyes and can't see a thing.

What is it?

10. Three Stars Riddle #10

When I take five and add six, I have eleven,

but when I take six and add seven, I have one.

What am I?

11. Three Stars Riddle #11

What goes through a door but never enters or exits?

Alone it holds on, but with its partner, it learns to let go?

12. Three Stars Riddle #12

To unravel me You need a simple key though not one made by locksmith's hand

This is a key that only you, and I, could ever understand.

A book a date or even a riddle would show what I have sealed

If you tell our secret then our future words revealed

13. Three Stars Riddle #13

I'm bit for your sake and held for mine

And if I'm silver you'll do just fine

What am I?

14. Three Stars Riddle #14

This mother comes from a family of eight

Supports her children in spite of their weight

Turns around without being called

Has held you since the time you crawled

15. Three Stars Riddle #15

I am the last line of defense on a rainy day

When I am severed, liquid I spray

If I am hit, color I change

And color, I come in quite a range

What I cover is very complex

And I keep it safe, since I'm easy to flex

16. Three Stars Riddle #16

I shift around, and am very slow

I don't move more than a few inches at a time

If I trip or lunge, down everything goes

It is simply my nature, though, I'm not unkind

What am I?

17. Three Stars Riddle #17

Walk on the living, they don't even mumble

Walk on the dead, they mutter and grumble

18. Three Stars Riddle #18

I am free the first time and second time

But the third time is going to cost you money

I am gifted to you by birth but can be stolen from you by honey?

What am I?

19. Three Stars Riddle #19

A book once owned by the wealthy, then easy to find

Once never for sale and often left behind

Now it is gone, lost to time

20. Three Stars Riddle #20

What goes further the slower it goes?

When it disappears everyone knows?

When you don't look at it, only then does it grow?

21. Three Stars Riddle #21

What is that which inflicts a scorch

that can lead to the creation of more sparks

but does not burn?

22. Three Stars Riddle #22

I cannot be felt or moved, and I will always be distant no matter how close you come

But don't fear, optimistic people will have you search me out anew

What am I?

23. Three Stars Riddle #23

We are emeralds and diamonds

Freed by the moon

Found by the sun

And picked up too soon

24. Three Stars Riddle #24

Looks like water, but it's deceit

Sits on sand, lays on concrete

People have been known

To chase it in desperation

But it gets them nowhere

And worsens their situation

25. Three Stars Riddle #25

I cannot be but what I am

Until the man who made me dies

Power and glory will fall to me finally

And those beneath me hope I am wise

26. Three Stars Riddle #26

We travel much, yet held in place, and close confined to boot

With any horse we will keep the pace, even if we are only on foot

What are they?

27. Three Stars Riddle #27

I move very slowly at an imperceptible rate

Although I take my time, I am never late

I accompany life, and survive past demise

I am viewed with esteem in many women's eyes

28. Three Stars Riddle #28

I can lead you to any home and any shop

I have seen every city, I go left and right

And matter what the weather is

I happily sleep outside at night!

29. Three Stars Riddle #29

The news is written on my face

I can take you any place

To a ship I am essential

But on a clear night I am inconsequential

30. Three Stars Riddle #30

I am a small room

And I contain very little air

Even if you find some common items in me

Many of my occupants are often rare

What am I?

31. Three Stars Riddle #31

I live on a busy street

If you want you can stand here for an hour or two

But if you show no signs of change I'll tell on you

32. Three Stars Riddle #32

My shallow hills are the faces of kings

My horizon is always near

My music sends men to the grave

My absence gives them fear

33. Three Stars Riddle #33

I stare at you, you stare at me

I have three eyes, yet cannot see

Every time I wink, I hand out commands

You do as you are told, with your feet and hands

What am I?

34. Three Stars Riddle #34

Weight in my stomach

Trees stick out my back

Nails hold my ribs in

And in the end, it's feet I lack

What am I?

35. Three Stars Riddle #35

Four jolly men sat down to play, they played all night until the break of day

They played more for cash than sake of fun, with a separate score for every one

When it came time to square accounts, they all made quite fair amounts

Not one lost and all gained, and not one cheater to be blamed

What were these men playing?

36. Three Stars Riddle #36

You can find them on plants

Most have two

Having one for music is a boon for you

Someone may ask you for yours and, politely, you will lend

And it you play by it, you are quite talented, friend

37. Three Stars Riddle #37

Isn't alive, yet can stand up

Can come out copper and end up as steel

So thin, a child could break one

But together they have the strength to pull a man

What is it?

38. Three Stars Riddle #38

A house of wood in a hidden place

Built without nails or tools

High above the earthen ground, keeps secrets safe

It holds pale gems of many hues

39. Three Stars Riddle #39

In this place, people lie, people cry, and people ask why

In this place people dig, people renege, and people promise to jig

In this place people sit, people admit, and people visit

In this place, people sleep, people weep, and people's solitude keep

What is it?

40. Three Stars Riddle #40

My sides are firmly laced about

Essentially nothing within

You'll think my head is strange indeed

Being nothing else but skin

41. Three Stars Riddle #41

I'm neither friend nor enemy, but I can mark your end

I am very small, but very tough

If you have me, then you have it rough

For when I am one, I learn to multiply

And it is from you that this knowledge was pried

42. Three Stars Riddle #42

I march before armies, a thousand salute me

My fall is a sign of victory, but no one would shoot me

The wind is my lover, beholder of my glory

I am regarded with fondness but my history can be gory

43. Three Stars Riddle #43

What is neither inside the house nor outside the house but a home

without some wouldn't be considered much of a home at all?

Chapter Four

Brain Teasers!

1. Hardware Store Math

A man went to the hardware store to do a little shopping

He looked over the prices and correctly deduced the following deductions:

1 would cost $.75

12 would cost $1.50

122 would cost $2.25

When he left the store he had spent $2.25, what did he buy?

2. The Amazing Race

A red car and a blue car participated in a two car race. The red car driver easily beats the blue car driver. How did the bias newspapers truthfully write their report to look as if the blue car driver did better?

3. The Sloth's Journey

A sloth fell out of its favorite tree. The tree is 30 feet tall. During day time, the sloth climbs 5 feet while at night when the sloth sleeps he slips back 4 feet. In how many days will the sloth make it back to the top of the tree?

4. Tom's Trial

Tom has been caught stealing gold from a mine, and is brought into town to see justice. The judge isn't one for killing and wants to show him some sympathy, but the law clearly calls for two shots to be taken at Tom from close range. To make things a little fairer for Tom, the judge tells him she will place two bullets into a six-chambered revolver, and they will be placed in two chambers right next to each other. She will spin the chamber, close it, and take one shot. If Tom is still alive, she will then either take another shot, or spin the chamber again before shooting, the choices is up to Tom.

The judge takes the first shot. Click! It was blank. Then the judge asks, "Do you want me to pull the trigger again, or should I spin the chamber a second time before pulling the trigger?"

What should Tom choose?

5. The Light Bulb and The Switch

Outside a room there are three light switches. One of switch is connected to a light bulb inside the room. Each of the three switches can be either 'ON' or 'OFF.'

You are allowed to set each switch the way you want it and then enter the room. But you can only enter the room one time.

How do you figure out which switch controls the light bulb?

6. The Clever Songsinger

A man is sitting in the lobby of a hotel, unable to afford a room. He sees the man next to him pull out several large bills to tip the bellhop and figures him to be quite rich. Feeling clever, he turns to the rich man and says to him, "I have an amazing talent; I know almost every song that has ever existed." The rich man laughs. The poor man says, "I am willing to bet you all the money you have in your wallet that I can sing a genuine song with a lady's name of your choice in it."

The rich man laughs again and says, "OK, how about my daughter's name, Lulu Ann Deebutaux?"

The rich man goes home poor. The poor man goes home rich. What song was sung?

7. The Hanged Man Mystery

The hanged man is found in a room with no windows and only a single door, which was locked from the inside. He hung himself from the only piece of ornamentation in the room, a chandelier. Beneath his feet is only a puddle of water. How did he hang himself?

8. The Length Doesn't Matter

You are given two ropes with variable dimensions. However, if we start burning both ropes, they will burn in exactly same amount of time: 1 hour. The ropes are uneven in length and composition. You are asked to measure 45 minutes by using these two ropes.

How can you do it?

Please note that you can't break the rope in half as the ropes do not burn in this fashion.

9. The Lonely Old Man

An old man lives alone in a flat. Because of his age, he is not able to move comfortably and has most of his needs delivered to his house. On Friday while delivering the mail, postman said he felt something was suspicious. Glancing through the window he saw the body of the old man. Police arrive on the scene. On the outside of flat, they found two bottles of milk, Tuesday newspaper, some unopened mail, and prepackaged meals. The police waste no time in arresting the culprit.

Who was the murderer?

10. The River Crossing Pt. 1

A man has to get a fox, a chicken, and a sack of corn across a river. He has a rowboat, and it is only big enough to fit him and one other thing. If the fox and the chicken are left together, the fox will eat the chicken. If the chicken and the corn are left together, the chicken will eat the corn.

How does the man get all three across?

11. The River Crossing Pt. 2

Four people need to cross a dark river at night. They have only one torch and the river is too dangerous to cross without the torch. If all people cross simultaneously the torch light won't be sufficient, so they must cross in groups of 2. Speed of each person crossing the river is different. Cross time for each person is, A can cross in 1 min, B in 2 minutes, C in 7 minutes, and D in 10 minutes.

What is the shortest time needed for all four of them to cross the river?

12. A Game of Marbles

Mark and Vince are playing a game. There are 11 marbles on the table and Mark and Vince get to pick marble(s) one by one with the following rules:

1. You need to pick at least one marble.

2. You can't pick more than five marbles.

The one that picks the last marble will lose. Mark starts the game.

How many marbles must Mark pick in order to make sure that he wins the game?

13. The Two Barbers

There are two barber shop in a small town – one located in the South End and the other on the North End. The shop in the South End is quite untidy and the barber has a shabby haircut. While the shop in the North End is quite neat and clean and the barber is sporting an excellent haircut himself.

Which of the two shops should someone from out of town go to?

14. An Honest Question

Shelly is an honest person who never speaks a lie. He thinks of a number among 1, 2, and 3. Now, you can ask him only one question, for which the answer you will receive will be in the form of yes, no, or he doesn't know. But he will reply only truthfully.

What question should you ask him?

15. The Smart Merchant

Tanner is a witty trader who trades delicious fruit. He travels from one place to another with three sacks, which can hold 30 fruits each. The sacks cannot hold more than 30 fruits. On his way, he has to pass through thirty check points and at each check point, he has to give one fruit for each sack to the authorities.

How many fruits remain after he goes through all the thirty check points?

16. The Daring Escape

Once there lived a king who did not allow anybody to leave the kingdom or any foreigners into his kingdom. There was only one bridge that connected his Kingdom with the outside world. A guard who was a sharpshooter was specially assigned for a lookout on the bridge. According to the orders, anyone trying to escape should be killed and anyone coming to his kingdom would be escorted back out back. To take rest, the guard used to sit inside his guardhouse on top of the bridge for 5 minutes and return back on the lookout. The bridge took a minimum of 8 minutes to cross over.

Even then, a woman was able to escape the kingdom without incurring any kind of harm to the guard. How?

17. The Confession Tape

Once there lived a king who did not allow anybody to leave the kingdom or any foreigners into his kingdom. There was only one bridge that connected his Kingdom with the outside world. A guard who was a sharpshooter was specially assigned for a lookout on the bridge. According to the orders, anyone trying to escape should be killed and anyone coming to his kingdom would be escorted back out back. To take rest, the guard used to sit inside his guardhouse on top of the bridge for 5 minutes and return back on the lookout. The bridge took a minimum of 8 minutes to cross over

Even then, a woman was able to escape the kingdom without incurring any kind of harm to the guard. How?

18. The Great Escape

Two world famous prisoners Laurence and Bird are locked in a cell. They want to escape from the cell. They can see an open window at 50 feet above the ground. Both of them stack everything in the cell but are never able to reach.

Then both of them decided to plan to escape by a tunnel and they start digging out.

After digging for just 5 days, Laurence and Bird figure out with the much easier plan than tunneling and they escape that night

How?

19. Colorful Friends

At a restaurant downtown, Mr. Red, Mr. Teal, and Mr. Grey meet for lunch. Under their coats they are wearing either a red, teal, or grey shirt. Mr. Teal says, "Hey, did you notice we are all wearing different colored shirts from our names?"

The man wearing the grey shirt says, "Wow, Mr. Teal, what an interesting observation."

Can you tell who is wearing what color shirt?

20. Time Test

Time in a digital clock can be palindromic (same when read forwards or backwards) like 12:21. What is the minimum interval between 2 times that are palindromic?

21. Change

I have 100 coins in my wallet. What is the minimum number of coins I would need in order to make sure each coin touched exactly three other coins.

22. Family Fishing Trip

Two fathers and their two sons go fishing together. They each catch one fish to take home with them. They do not lose any fish, and yet when they arrive at home they only have three fish. How can this be?

23. Too Many Times

You want to boil a two-minute egg. If you only have a three-minute timer and a five-minute timer can you boil the egg for only two minutes?

24. Water Balloon Fight

You are playing with water balloons with two other people, Frank and Sally. You're standing in a triangle and you all take turns throwing at one of the others of your choosing until there is only one person remaining. You have a 30% chance of hitting someone you aim at.

Frank has a 50/50 chance, and Sally always hits no matter what. If you hit somebody they are out and no longer get a turn. If the order of throwing is you, Frank, then Sally; what should you do to have the best chance of winning?

25. Enlightened Inheritance

An old man wanted to leave all of his money to one of his three sons, but he didn't know which one he should give it to. He gave each of them two coins and told them to buy something that would be able to fill their living room. The first man bought hay, but there was not enough to fill the room. The second bought a bundle of sticks, but he still could not fill the room. The third man bought two things that filled the room, so he obtained his father's fortune. What were the two things that the man bought?

26. Crossing The Line

Chandra is traveling by ship from south of the equator to the north. She has a cabin which has a bathroom, but no window. Chandra has no mapping instruments to give her any information. Yet, without leaving her room or talking with anyone, Chandra knew when the ship had crossed the equator. How did she know?

27. Treasure Trove

There are three chests, each of which contains 100 coins. One chest has 100 gold coins, one has 100 silver coins, and the third has an equal split of 50 gold coins and 50 silver coins.

Each chest is labeled, but all are labeled incorrectly. You are allowed to pick one coin from just one of the chests and after this you must correctly identify each of the three chests.

28. The Prisoner's Dilemma

There were 3 prisoners that were locked up. Two of them had perfect vision but the third prisoner was completely blind.

One day, the Warden gathered the prisoners together and said to them, "I have 5 hats. 2 of the hats are red and 3 are white. I will blindfold each of you and then put one of the hats on each of your heads. I will then put the remaining two hats in another room. Next, I will remove your blindfolds. At this point you may look at your fellow prisoners but may not speak to them. The person that can tell me the color of the hat on his head will go free. If you try and guess and are wrong, you shall have 20 years added to your sentence."

The hats were then placed on the prisoners' heads and the blindfolds were removed.

The Warden then spoke to the first prisoner, "What is the color of the hat on your head?" The prisoner looked around carefully but finally, not wanting to punished for guessing, said that he did not know.

The Warden then spoke to the second prisoner, "What is the color of the hat on your head?" This prisoner also looked carefully at the hats upon the heads of the other two prisoners, but finally admitted that he also did not know.

At this point, the Warden turned and began to walk away, assuming that the third prisoner who was blind could not know possibly the answer to the riddle.

But then the blind man spoke. "Excuse me," he said, "But I am certain my hat is white."

Surprised, the Warden turned around. He saw that the blind man was correct and ordered him to be freed at once.

How did the blind prisoner know the color of his hat?

29. Protecting Your Basket

I left my campsite and walked south for 2 miles. Then I turned east and hiked for 2 miles. I then turned north and hiked for 2 miles, at which time I came upon a bear sitting in my camp eating all of my food! What color was the bear?

30. Tricky Work

2 men catch 2 fish in 2 minutes. At this rate, how many men could catch 500 fish in 500 minutes?

31. A Jump, Skip, and a Hop

How can you place a pencil on the floor so that no one can jump over it?

32. The Bet

Henry places two very small glasses and two very large glasses onto separate sides of the table. He sets the very small glasses in front of his friend Gwen. The very small glasses take 3 seconds to drink and the very large glasses take 30 seconds. Henry fills all four glasses with water. He bets Gwen that he can finish his two very large glasses before she finishes her two very small ones. He has some stipulations, though.

They aren't allowed to touch each other's glasses at all. And Henry is given one glass head start. Gwen is allowed to drink once Henry's first glass hits the table. Knowing she will still have plenty of time, Gwen agrees to the bet. Moments later, Gwen has lost. How?

33. Mystery Bag

Miles and Wren are in a flat field. They both have packs on. Wren is dead. Miles is alive. Miles pack is open, Wren has his pack closed. What is in the packs?

34. Milk Honey

Throckmorten is a father with 9 sons. He also has 81 cows labeled as 1 through 81. The cows were labeled based on the amount of milk they produce. Cow 1 gives 1-liter of milk, Cow 2 gives 2 liters of milk and so on.

Throckmorten wants to distribute his 81 cows among all his sons such that each of them gets the same number of cows and access to the same quantity of milk.

35. The Heist

The famous thief, The Lightning Bug, and his team, need to break the safe to finish a secret job in exactly five minutes. They got just one chance at the job and then the local police will be informed.

They have following clues about the safe's combination:

1st Clue: Exactly one number is perfectly placed.

7 2 5

2nd clue: Everything is incorrect.

7 3 8

3rd clue: Two numbers are part of the code of the safe, but are wrongly placed.

4 7 6

4th clue: One number is part of the code of the safe, but is wrongly placed.

5 8 1

5th clue: One number is part of the code of the safe, but is wrongly placed.

1 2 6

36. Sweet Treats

Marcel brings 1000 candies for his sister, Jen, along with 10 boxes. Marcel asks Jen to place the candies in the boxes in a manner that if he asks for any number of candies, she can give him either a single box or a combination of boxes without taking any out. If she can do it, all 1000 candies will be hers.

How should she separate the candies in order to win them all?

37. Murderous Intent

Before going to work, Inspector Hash got into the fight with his wife. After coming back from work he found out that the police were in his home and his wife had just killed an intruder.

She told the police she killed the intruder in self-defense. She said she heard the door open and thought it was her husband. But as soon as she went to greet him, the burglar jumped out at her. She was so scared that she killed intruder immediately by stabbing him with a knife.

Inspector Hash asked the police to arrest his wife with conspiracy to commit murder.

Why?

38. A Pair to Roll

You are provided with two 6-sided dice. You have a complete liberty to mark any number from 0 to 9 on the faces of both die. You are tasked with being able to show every day on a calendar, 1 through 31, using only the two dice you have marked.

What numbers will you write on the dice?

39. Fibbing Friend

Two friends, Tim and Jim were talking about their family histories. Tim told some great stories about his courageous grandfather who fought for Britain in World War I.

Tim told Jim that his grandfather is so brave that he was awarded a bravery honor medal with words. "For Your Courage In Battle In World War I" embedded in to it.

Jim Knows that his friend is lying. How?

40. A Last Request

A man was found guilty of committing treason. As per the rules of the empire, the king sentenced him to death. However, he gave the man a choice; a choice to decide which way he wanted to die. The man was quite smart and he said something, which saved him from his death.

What did he say?

41. Enough to Go Around

You have a solid bar of dark chocolate bar. It's size is 2 x 8 squares. You need to break it and get 1 x 1 square pieces of that chocolate. If you can break that bar only along its length or breadth, how many times will you have to break to get the 1 x 1 pieces?

42. A Yummy Deal

A candy shop owner allows customers to purchase a sweet in exchange of five wrappers of the same sweet. The local school children decide to work as a team to get the most candy. Together, they consumed 77 sweets in a month.

How many sweets can they get for all their wrappers?

43. Taking the Lead

An item is made from iron blocks in a lathe shop. Each block is enough for 1 item. Iron shavings accumulated for making 6 items can be melted and made into a block. How many items can be made from 36 blocks.

44. Fractions

Use these digits once each only to compose two fractions, which when added together equal 1.

0,1,2,3,4,5,6,7,8,9

45. A Shared Meal

A shepherd met two bakers, one of whom had three loaves and the other had five loaves. All the loaves were the same size. The three men agreed to share the eight loaves equally between them. After they had eaten, the shepherd gave the bakers eight coins as payment for his meal.

How should the two bakers divide this money so it is most fair?

46. Feeling A Little Horse

A farmer has three sick horses. She has a 24 oz bottle of medicine and needs to give each horse eight ounces of the medicine. She is a rural farmer and is unable to get to the store. She has only three clean containers, which measure 5, 11, and 13 fluid ounces. She has no way of heating water to wash the containers and doesn't want to spread germs.

How can she divide the medicine to give each horse an equal portion without having any two horses drink from the same container?

47. The Last Puzzle

An old woman was rather fond of riddles so she left a trick in her will for her daughter. When the old woman died, her will stipulated that her estate was to be liquidated and a check was to be written for the full amount. The check was to be placed in one of three envelopes. The other two envelopes would contain a blank piece of paper. If the daughter could determine from the writing on the envelopes, stipulated in the will, which envelope contained the check, she would inherit her mother's fortune.

Otherwise, the fortune would go to the old woman's favorite charity for sick cats. The daughter had to choose the envelope based on the writing alone. The daughter was told that only one envelope had a true statement written upon it. The other two had statements that were false.

The envelopes were labeled as follows: 1. This envelope does not have the check 2. This envelope has the check 3. The second envelope does not have the check.

Which envelope should the daughter pick?

48. Look Both Ways

Two cars were involved in an accident in the center of town. One car was small and green and the other was long and black. Everyone found in the green car, including the driver, was unharmed. The driver of the long black car was fine, but there was one dead man in the back.

The driver of the green car was found at fault for the accident. No foul play or ill intent was suspected of anyone and the driver of the green car was not charged for the death, why?

49. Throwing Your Weight Around

Jessie has 8 cinder blocks, 7 of them weigh the same amount and one is slightly heavier. Using a balance scale, how can Jessie find the heavier block in just two weighings?

50. Compost Composure

A gardener combined 4 compost heaps with 6 others. How many compost heaps does he have?

51. Half Empty or Half Full

Six cups are in a row. The first three are full of milk; the second three are empty. By moving only one cup, can you arrange them so empty and full cups alternate?

52. Sock Options

If your sock drawer has 12 red socks, 8 blue socks, 16 orange socks, and 4 black socks, how many socks would you have to pull out in the dark to be sure you had a matching pair?

53. What's in a Name?

If all Woots are Curlies, all Bobbins are Kukes, no Hoppers are Bobbins, and all Curlies are Bobbins, is it true that all Bobbins are Curlies?

54. Drink Up?

Two women ate dinner together. They both ordered ice tea. One woman was very thirsty and drank them very fast. She drank five of them in all. In the same amount of time, the other woman drank one and a half glasses of ice tea.

The woman who drank one and a half died while the other survived. It was later found that all of the drinks were poisoned. Why did the other woman survive?

55. Well Planned Punishment

A teacher decides to give a pop quiz one day. All of her students are close and know each other. So they refuse to take the quiz as a group, thinking that the teacher will call off the quiz. She can only give one student detention for skipping the quiz. The teacher knows if a student hears they will get a detention they take the quiz instead.

How can she threaten her students with the single detention so they all take the quiz?

56. A Big Suprise

There is a ball where 100 high-powered politicians are coming as guests. All of them are either honest or liars. You walk in knowing two things:

a) At least one of them is honest.

b) If you take any two politicians, at least one of them is a liar.

From this information, can you know how many are liars and how many are honest?

57. Bits and Pieces

You are in a room with two metal rods and no other metal. One of them is magnetized and the other is not. How can you determine which one is magnetized and which is not?

58. Assigned Seating

In a field there are some flowers with some bees hovering over those flowers.

How many flowers and how many bees if both of the following statements are true: 1) If each bee lands on a flower, one bee doesn't get a flower. 2) If two bees share each flower there is one flower left out.

59. Blind Investment

There are 100 coins scattered in a dark room. 90 have heads facing up and 10 are facing tails up. You cannot tell which coins are which since it is too dark to see. How would you sort the coins in to two piles that contain the same number of tails up coins?

60. Thief Among Us

A man accidentally leaves a $100 dollar bill on his desk and leaves work. When he returns the money is gone. He has three suspects: the salesman, the HR Representative, and the mail guy. The Salesman says when he found it he put the money under a book on the man's desk to keep it safe. They check and it is no longer there. The HR

Representative says she moved it when she was cleaning to the inside of the book between page 3 and 4. They open the book and look between page number 1 and 2 but it isn't there. The mail guy says he saw it sticking out of the book and to keep it safe he moved it to between page number 4 and 5.

Once they are done the culprit is promptly arrested. Who did it and how did he know?

61. The Trick In The Bottle

Philip put a coin in a bottle and put a cork on the bottle and later managed to get the coin out without taking out the cork or breaking the bottle.

How did he do it?

62. Tree House

A house is built above a river between two trees. It is attached to the middle of the two tree's trunks. The river rises by 2 inches each year, but the trees grow 1 inch each year. If the house is 4 inches above the river how long will it take for water to hit the house?

63. Paint Job

John has been hired to paint the numbers 1 through 100 on 100 rooms in a hotel.

How many times with he have to paint 8?

64. Royal Decree

Everyday a farmer must pay the king one pound of gold and leave it on a collection plate in front of his house. Every morning the sheriff comes by to make sure he has put a pound of gold on the plate. The king collects the gold every six days from the plate. If the form only has one six pound block of gold, how can he make only two parallel cuts and still follow the kings rules each day?

65. Bitter Pill to Swallow

You have a disease but thankfully there is a medicine for it. Every day you must take one pill called BTZ and one pill called CTZ. One day, you pour one BTZ in your hand then you pour two CTZs in your hand by accident. These pills are identical and if you take too much or too little of either pill on any day you will die. You cannot get a refill or throw any pills away.

How can you still take the pills you have in your hand and live?

66. The Chess Master

A man challenges the greatest chess playing computer in the world to two games of chess. He guarantees that he will win or tie at least one of the games for sure. His only condition is they play both games at the same time. The programmers of the computer agree to the contest.

How does he guarantee he wins or ties at least one game?

67. Happy Birthday

A man named Jack was born on December 21st, yet his birthday is during the summer this year. How is that possible?

68. Not to Marry

An evil king finds a woman he wants to marry but she refuses. The king gives her a deal: he will write 'YES' and 'NO' on two pieces of paper. The papers will be put into a box and she will choose one.

If it says yes she will marry him, if it says no she will not. The only problem is that the king cheats and puts two pieces of paper that say yes in the box, everyone knows this, but none dare speak against the king.

What can the woman do?

69. Cabin in the Woods

Four hikers are forced in to a pitch black cabin by a bad storm. On the door of the cabin is a sign that reads, "Come in as you please, but fall asleep and you will die".

The hikers all take this very seriously and devise a plan so they can stay awake. They all stand in a corner and one person walks from one corner along the wall to the next and taps the person in that corner making sure they are awake. They do this for many hours until one hiker suddenly has a realization and runs out of the cabin screaming, quickly followed by the others.

Why did they run out terrified?

70. To the Races

A racetrack needs to submit its 3 fastest horses to the World Championship Horse race out of 25 horses. However, due to a computer error, all of their information was lost and they don't know any of the horse's times.

They can only race 5 horses at once. So, what is the fewest number of races they can conduct to find the 3 fastest horses?

Chapter Five

Four Stars Riddle

1. Four Stars Riddle #1

My sorrow, a life measured in hours

I can only serve my master by being devoured

I am faster thin But my master likes me fat and slow

A gentle wind can be my greatest foe

2. Four Stars Riddle #2

At the sound of me, some may scream and stamp their feet

At the sound of me, many often laugh and weep

I am all of your emotions, and I am no one

I can be serious and I can be fun

What am I?

3. Four Stars Riddle #3

Grasping stiffly for the sky

I bare my fingers when it's cold

In warmth I wear a verdant glove

And as it cools I dress in gold

What Am I?

4. Four Stars Riddle #4

Soft and fragile is my body, I get my food in earth and mud

I'm the danger hidden in beauty, for if not careful, I draw blood

What am I?

5. Four Stars Riddle #5

An iron horse with a flaxen tail

The faster the horse runs

The shorter his tail becomes

What is it?

6. Four Stars Riddle #6

We aren't always intended to harm

On occasion can be used to charm

But our venom has been known to change lives

It is up to you to sort our truth from our lies

7. Four Stars Riddle #7

What never asks questions but is often answered?

Fixes a knock but isn't a tool

What prompts repetition will make you run faster

And callers disappearance will make you the fool?

8. Four Stars Riddle #8

I drift forever with the current down these long canals of copper and gold

Tame, yet wild, I run elusive, or so I am told

Before I came, the world was darker, colder, sometimes, rougher, true

But though I might make living easy, I'm good at killing too

9. Four Stars Riddle #9

As a pit inside a tree, I'll help your words have gravity

I advise not to use me up too fast, the more I move the less I last

10. Four Stars Riddle #10

What moves across the land but never has to steer?

Quick as a bullet, can get you far and near

It lets out a shout to make sure it is heard

For its forward momentum will not be deterred

11. Four Stars Riddle #11

I have a frame but my pictures are up to you

I have poles but you are my support

What am I?

12. Four Stars Riddle #12

No one knows my beginning, middle or end

And all the greatest thinkers see it but can't comprehend

What am I?

13. Four Stars Riddle #13

Almost everyone sees me without noticing me

For I am always the portal and rarely the desire itself

14. Four Stars Riddle #14

What starts in a field and then crushed in to dust

Thrown in to fire, it turns the color of rust?

Risen again, hot and anew

It must be broken to share between me and you?

15. Four Stars Riddle #15

I am a guardian and I sit on a bridge

My ward can see right through me

While others wonder what I hide

What am I?

16. Four Stars Riddle #16

I'm a slippery fish in a cloudy sea

You need neither hook nor spear to capture me

With your hand you'll hunt down this fish

To make sure that it ends up in the dish

17. Four Stars Riddle #17

My uses are changing, but I still remain the same

My interior is quiet, and stories are my game

I am timeless, a promise of knowledge to be shared

All you need do is ask, and my secret are freely bared

18. Four Stars Riddle #18

Hidden in dark and sometimes bright

I float among the twinkling lights

Oceans and waves obey my call

yet mountains I cannot move at all

My face wide and round and kind

and my beauty brings poetry to mind

19. Four Stars Riddle #19

Everyone needs it to live, that said, you are still encouraged to give

It's easy for you to lose some, but too much and it can be gruesome

Don't worry if a little is lost, on your own you can remake the cost

What is it?

20. Four Stars Riddle #20

Crooked as a rainbow, and slick as a plate

Shiny like a mirror, Nothing can yank it straight

21. Four Stars Riddle #21

What has wings, but cannot fly

Is enclosed, but can outside also lie

Is the place of kings and queens

And person of every means

What is it upon which I can stand?

Which can lead us to different lands

22. Four Stars Riddle #22

A mile from end to end

Yet as close to you as a friend

A precious commodity, freely given

Seen on the dead as well as the living

Found on the rich, poor, short and tall

But shared among children most of all

What is it?

23. Four Stars Riddle #23

I can hiss like bacon, but I am from an egg

I have plenty of backbone, but lack a good leg

I peel layers like onions, but still remain whole

I can be long like a pole, and yet fit in a hole

What am I?

24. Four Stars Riddle #24

Useful tool for those in darkness dwell

Within you, corrupting like a deadly spell

Best served in a toast held with friends

Eye your glass or it'll be your own end

25. Four Stars Riddle #25

An open ended barrel, but it's shaped like a hive

It is filled with the flesh, and the flesh is alive!

26. Four Stars Riddle #26

I saw a man round in form, and looked quite bold

He was dressed very warm, and he stood in the cold

And when he felt the sun, he started to run, and he disappeared, all things told

Who was this man?

27. Four Stars Riddle #27

If you are the only one who knows of it, it is useless to you

The more people you tell in your desperation, the less likely people are to believe you

28. Four Stars Riddle #28

If you like pretty jewels that sparkle and shine

I invite you to dig in and take a look at mine

My first is purple, fit for royalty

My second is green, where Dorothy needed to be

My third is red, a July birthday fan

My fourth is seen in strings and made up of sand

My fifth is hardest, too expensive for me

My sixth is Crocodolite, and looks like what big cats use to see

Seventh has a first and a last, a man-made type of April's stone

Eighth is a rainbow and must be carefully hone

Now you know all my treasures

In this earth you'll find none better

29. Four Stars Riddle #29

One tooth to bite

He is forest forged and forests foe

One tooth to fight

As the mightiest of warriors might know

30. Four Stars Riddle #30

I have no wings but I fly

I am not a fly but I bite

And if you bite me

Your task is one people will pity

31. Four Stars Riddle #31

Not chest or box is now discussed

Money can be held in it but not riches alone

If it is ever pushed to be tested

then what was held is now lost for good

32. Four Stars Riddle #32

Had by all but seen by few

I'm on the inside and on the out, even with you

Though there is many who'd have you doubt

33. Four Stars Riddle #33

Job and Joan were found on the ground gasping for air surrounded by glass and water. The person who found them quickly got a bowl of water for them and they were fine. What happened to Job and Joan?

34. Four Stars Riddle #34

Crawls over pages and fells wild beasts

Crafted from feather, wood, and ink

Helps guide you home and through unfamiliar streets

A tool with a partner that it shares a link

35. Four Stars Riddle #35

You can easily touch me, but not see me

You can throw me out, but not away

You keep me straight for proper manners

If someone has me, then you want to keep them close

36. Four Stars Riddle #36

Some use me, while others do not

Some remember what others have forgot

For gain or aid, I'm can be expertly

But I can't be easily found or tossed into the sea

Only gained through patience and time

You can even use me to unravel this rhyme?

37. Four Stars Riddle #37

You can play me and pull me

I'm especially fond of the naive

I'm enjoyable to give

But frustrating to receive

38. Four Stars Riddle #38

I am more then all my parts

I can be made of steel and of heart

While held, I am hard to cut and tear

But without being tense, no weight I can bear

39. Four Stars Riddle #39

Break it and it sets immediately

Only for someone to come along and try and break it again while all watch and applaud.

40. Four Stars Riddle #40

He was tricked in to a cage. When a woman sees him, she is very pleased, smiling at his current predicament. She would let him out where he would have no way of finding his way back. This was all perfectly legal. What's going on?

41. Four Stars Riddle #41

I am red on inside and red on the out

And from limb tips I sprout.

I cradle a stone inside my breast

And you'll find me atop the day of rest

42. Four Stars Riddle #42

What tree that definitely grows and grows but does not have a shadow?

You benefit from the fruit it bears, but you can never ever eat it?

43. Four Stars Riddle #43

Screaming across the pitch black skies

A celebrations raucous conclusion

Yet moments later, my outburst through

I am naught but an after-illusion

44. Four Stars Riddle #44

Belt of water, tongue of wood

Skin of stone, for long I've stood

My fingers short, stretch towards the sky

Inside my bosom, men live their lives

45. Four Stars Riddle #45

It has no top or bottom

no beginning middle or end

It can hold flesh, bones, and blood

While still allowing it to bend

46. Four Stars Riddle #46

I can be made useful readily

I am a rock, shell, and bone medley

If I was made into a man, I'd make people dream

I am gathered in my millions by ocean, sea, and stream.

47. Four Stars Riddle #47

Used on a diamond and left on a board

It's great for a gymnast his grip to restore

Put it up if you have an excuse

Use it on the streets and hope you don't lose.

What is it?

48. Four Stars Riddle #48

I tremble at each breath of air

And yet can heaviest burdens bear

I usually go with the flow

But don't break my tension and it's your woe.

49. Four Stars Riddle #49

My first master had four legs, my second has two

My first I serve in life, my second I serve after I die

Durable I am, yet soft beside

Against ladies cheeks I often reside.

Chapter Six

Five Stars Riddle

1. Five Stars Riddle #1

If you break me I may not mend

but I can be broken again

If you touch me, I may be snared

But if once broken I will be scared

If you lose me, nothing will matter

But most things are matters of me

2. Five Stars Riddle #2

Five hundred begins it, five hundred ends it

Five in the middle is seen

The Leader of letters, the oldest of numbers

Take up their stations with five in-between

Join all together, and then you will bring

Before you the name of an eminent king

3. Five Stars Riddle #3

Three brothers share a family sport: A non-stop marathon of an everyday sort

The oldest one is stocky and slow, And trudges determinedly onward he'll go

The middle brother's tall and limber, the click of his pace the most noticeable timbre

The youngest runs with energy to the brim, few runners you'll lose track of as quickly as him

"He'll have his fun, we let him run," both brothers quietly sigh. "Though he's surely the fastest one, he's really second, poor guy."

4. Five Stars Riddle #4

When you went in to the woods, you caught me

You hated me, yet you needed to search for me

You brought me home because you couldn't find me

What am I?

5. Five Stars Riddle #5

I take what you has been given to you and surrender everything else by waving my flag

6. Five Stars Riddle #6

Thousands hoard gold within this house, but no man has yet laid hands upon it

Spears past counting guard this house, But no man takes up arms for it

7. Five Stars Riddle #7

The land was white, the seed was black. Thought was sown and wisdom harvested.

What is it?

8. Five Stars Riddle #8

A thousand colored folds stretch toward the sky, Atop a tender strand

Rising from the earth on high, Til killed by maiden's hand

9. Five Stars Riddle #9

Where I am from the sky is orange and the windows are red, I feast on violet bananas and the dine on blue oranges. Where am I?

10. Five Stars Riddle #10

It holds more knowledge than one mind can

But can easily crumple in your hand

Can hold every color you can see

But would have a hard time keeping you from me

11. Five Stars Riddle #11

I'm in a box, full of that which is most rare

Though indestructible, I am treated with care

I'm a thieves dream, a delight to hock

While dull in the dirt, I glisten once unlocked

12. Five Stars Riddle #12

My voice is tender, my waist is slender and I'm often invited to play

Though wherever I go, I must take a bow or else I have nothing to say

What am I?

13. Five Stars Riddle #13

In marble halls as white as milk

Lined with a skin as soft as silk

Cradled in a fountain clear

A golden treasure does appear

No doors there are to this hold

Though many break in for the gold

14. Five Stars Riddle #14

I'm sometimes white and told I'm wrong

I can break a heart and hurt the strong

I can build up love or tear it down

I can forge a smile or bring a frown

15. Five Stars Riddle #15

All about the house, with this lady you dance

Yet it is always for work, and never romance

She takes no offense, for that is the plan

To make your home spick and span

16. Five Stars Riddle #16

I do not think or eat or slumber

I do not run or fear thunder

Just like you, I look the same

But I don't age or ever change

17. Five Stars Riddle #17

Though it is not a bull, it has horns

Though it is not a mule, it has a packed saddle

And wherever it goes it leaves a sign to mark its passage

18. Five Stars Riddle #18

Comes in bits and pieces, put together forms a whole

It is gymnastics for the mind, the more you think, the more you find

Sometimes it can be a grind, but then, that is the goal

19. Five Stars Riddle #19

Held by the world, linked with its fate

Has missed every day but seen every date

Was there for the dawn of man, or so I am told

And yet is never more than 5 weeks old?

20. Five Stars Riddle #20

You might just see me in the mirror

Or in the things you crave

But if you let me grow too large

I might make you misbehave

21. Five Stars Riddle #21

They can be harbored, but few hold water

You can nurse them, but only by holding them against someone else

You carry them, but not with your arms

You can bury them, but not in the ground

22. Five Stars Riddle #22

Some are quick to take them. Others must be coaxed

Those who choose to take it gain and lose the most

It is always the ones who take them and win

Who will be lured back again

23. Five Stars Riddle #23

A natural state, I'm sought by all

Go without me, and you shall fall

To find me you may need a scale

Work from a guess and you'll often fail

You should use me when you wish to spend

But it is often too late once this is kenned

24. Five Stars Riddle #24

I can bring tears to your eyes

And friends to your side

Make you laugh

And change history on your behalf

Keeping hold of me is serious business

But you'll never notice you lost me until it Is too late

What am I?

25. Five Stars Riddle #25

I used to fill rooms but now I'm flat

I can build a tall tower or fold in half

I have tons of sills

I like to show off my fruit

And if I get injured

I just need a good boot

26. Five Stars Riddle #26

I give refuge in exchange for sight

Though I may negotiate if you bring your own light

Whether or not you can see

Will not silence my mimicry

27. Five Stars Riddle #27

After you go through a fall I will take over

All life will stall, or at least grow slower

The thaw that follows is met was song

Then you'll have to wait a while since for me, since the days are too long

What am I?

28. Five Stars Riddle #28

I can be flipped, looped, and broken but I rarely move

I can be closed, opened, and sometimes removed

I am sealed by hands, by words, and by ink

I can be as long as a book or as short as a wink

What am I?

29. Five Stars Riddle #29

Living, I cannot truly exist

But in death I am an inspiration

You always doubt me

But to reject me means to reject your roots

I am what is passed from old to young

To make sure that the lessons of the past are never forgotten

What am I?

30. Five Stars Riddle #30

I am unseen but all people know of me

Only in apathy of others can I continue to be

I am intangible yet sharper than any sword

If I'm slain it would save the world

I come from nothingness but can fell even the mightiest kings

And yet my down fall can come from the most everyday things

31. Five Stars Riddle #31

A precious stone, as clear as glass

Seek it out after the longest days are passed

You can walk on water with its power

Try to keep hold of it, and it'll vanish in an hour

32. Five Stars Riddle #32

Consumer of iron, destroyer of steel

I force the towers of man to kneel

Brought by the weather, nurtured by time

I cause concern, but not fear, when you see my signs

33. Five Stars Riddle #33

I always follow my brother but you cannot see me, only him

He leads the charge with vigor and vim

I lead my brother and you can hear him and not me

But his voice always speaks for both of us

What are we?

34. Five Stars Riddle #34

People are hired to get rid of me

I'm often drifting under your bed

Futile, I always return, you see

Bite me and they will pronounce you dead

35. Five Stars Riddle #35

Mine belong to me; Yours belong to you

But sharing them is what make our friendship true

They can make you feel happy or make you feel blue

They never end until the day you do

36. Five Stars Riddle #36

Though I have no means of locomotion

My main use is on the go

Although I cannot speak

I tell you what you want to know

I am named for what you'll do to me, not what I do for you

Though when others ask for me, they'll name my use to you

Chapter Seven

Six Stars Riddle

1. Six Stars Riddle #1

I'm weepy-eyed but not a crier

Silver-tongued, but never liar

Double-winged, but not much a flier

Air-cooled, but I'll never get drier

2. Six Stars Riddle #2

I have a body without blood

I have a tongue and yet no head

I was buried before I was born

And I cry for everyone except for the dead.

3. Six Stars Riddle #3

I have branches but my green stays hidden

Safe inside but you might not trust me

I hold up trusts but that may divide us

And when we finally split, no account remains to testify to it

What am I?

4. Six Stars Riddle #4

Stealthy as a shadow in the dead of night

Cunning, I show my affection with a bite

Never owned but often carried

My victims on display, never buried

5. Six Stars Riddle #5

To give me to someone I don't belong to is cowardly

To take me can be noble but also foolhardy

I can be a game, but one without winners

I am less interested in the sins than I am the sinners

What am I?

6. Six Stars Riddle #6

Though I make you weak at the worst of times

I may keep you safe, I can even be wise

I make your hands shake

And your heart race

I can hold anyone firmly in their place

7. Six Stars Riddle #7

I am your window and your lamp

I can be both clouded and shining

I am a gem set in marbled white

I fill with water and overflow

I lay you bare, but I cannot say a word

8. Six Stars Riddle #8

I can be born in anger or bred in fear

But finally forged in word and deed

When comes a time that I'm called forth

I come to serve those most in need

I am praised more than practiced

Held as code and tested in mettle

Barked at when things are tense

But high held when matters are settled

9. Six Stars Riddle #9

I cut through evil

With my double edged sword

And chaos flees at my blinding rays

I can be born from upheaval

But from my balance fair law is born

Though such a state will never meet my gaze

What am I?

10. Six Stars Riddle #10

A hundred brothers lie next to each other

Each white and fine and supported by one spine

I am the thin finger that lies between just two

Remove me to gather their wisdom to you

11. Six Stars Riddle #11

When you do not know what I am, then I am something

But when you know what I am, then I am nothing

I often rhyme, but sometimes poorly

And I am often a simile, metaphorically

What am I?

12. Six Stars Riddle #12

Different lights make me strange

For each one my size will change

I am clad in several colors

Some a bit more common than others

And if you wish to charm and flatter

Then I am a popular subject matter

13. Six Stars Riddle #13

Having one means having something to follow

Once you question it, it could mean you lose it

People seek it, if they do they are probably lost

You can be given one

But some will try and give you one that suits them better than it does
you

What is it?

14. Six Stars Riddle #14

I am the outstretched hand that seizes hold of the wind

Wisdom flows through me from other's hands

I hold your head while you dream your dreams

My gentlest touch brings people to their knees with laughter

What am I?

15. Six Stars Riddle #15

A burden for more than just its weight and daily carried out

He who takes it wishes it had never come about

It can given to those who don't deserve it by the cruel

But only called in to question when it is unusual

16. Six Stars Riddle #16

There is one, and there is always another, for without the other, the one wouldn't be one at all.

17. Six Stars Riddle #17

Slayer of regrets, old and new

Sought by many, found by few

Attempt to bought but must be earned

It is the thing for which only the truly remorseful yearn

Conclusion

You made it to the end. All that lies beyond this point is the answer to the first riddle of the book. If you have made it this far, you know all the answers. Either you solved them or you looked at the end of each chapter, and either way is fine.

That is the one thing about riddles, what you know you cannot unknow.

But remember, each riddle you remember is one you can share with others. So even if cannot experience the challenge of solving it ever again you now have the joy of sharing it with others.

I hope you found these riddles as satisfying to solve for you as they were for me to assemble. Good luck, future riddler.

And finally, the answer to the riddle in the introduction:

Chess

Answers

Chapter One: One Star Riddle

1. A Coffin

2. Sand

3. Counterfeit Money

4. Soap

5. One

6. The sun

7. A flag (Time is also an acceptable answer)

8. Silence

9. A map

10. The catcher (In a baseball game)

11. Birthday

12. Eating watermelon

13. Snow

14. A six sided die

15. A desert

16. A volcano

17. Vowels

18. A ski lift

19. Do you mind?

20. Gold

21. Rain

22. The news

23. A knife

24. A cartoon

25. An apple

26. A banana

27. Red

28. Chess pieces

29. Movie theater

30. A worm

31. A sock

32. They are beds

33. The tongue

34. Hair

35. A thumb drive

36. Bark

37. They were hurricanes

38. An arrow

39. A deck of cards

40. A match

41. A typewriter

Chapter Two: Two Stars Riddle

1. A river

2. An iceberg

3. Your reflection

4. Fingernails

5. Footsteps

6. An anchor

7. A plate

8. A nose

9. A skull

10. A keyboard

11. A net

12. A camera

13. A mirror

14. A newspaper

15. A cavity

16. A windmill

17. A grandfather clock

18. The Earth

19. A newspaper

20. A glacier

21. A wheelbarrow

22. A seesaw

23. A tombstone

24. An icicle

25. A bridge

26. Sawdust

27. The ocean

28. A coin

29. An echo

30. A black hole

31. A stamp

32. A picture frame

33. Frost

34. A drawbridge

35. Four

36. The telephone

37. The tide

38. A lock

39. A lighthouse

40. A kite

41. Salt

42. An asteroid

43. A tornado

Chapter Three: Three Stars Riddle

1. Stove, fire, and smoke

2. A shadow

3. Sand in an hourglass

4. An ace (in a deck of cards)

5. A fish

6. A wheel

7. Scissors

8. A sailing ship

9. A button

10. A clock

11. A keyhole

12. A cipher

13. A tongue

14. The Earth

15. Skin

16. A tectonic plate

17. Leaves

18. Teeth

19. A phone book

20. Money

21. Ink

22. The horizon

23. Dew

24. A mirage

25. A prince

26. Spurs

27. Hair

28. A street

29. A compass

30. A refrigerator

31. A parking meter

32. Coins

33. A traffic light

34. A sailing ship

35. Instruments

36. An ear

37. Hair

38. A nest

39. A cemetery

40. A drum

41. Virus

42. A flag

43. Windows

Chapter Four: Brain Teaser!

1. House numbers

2. The newspaper reported (correctly) that the red car came in next to last while the blue car came in second.

3. 26 days

In 25 days, he will climb 25 feet and the next five feet will take him to the top of the tree.

4. Tom should have The judge pulled the trigger again without spinning.

We know that the first chamber the judge fired was one of the four empty chambers. Since the bullets were placed one right after the other, one of the empty chambers is followed by a bullet, and the other three empty chambers are followed by another empty chamber. So if Tom has the judge pull the trigger again, the probability that a bullet will be fired is 1/4.

If the judge spins the chamber again, the probability that she shoots Tom would be two out of six, or 1/3, since there are two possible bullets that would be in firing position out of the six possible chambers that would be in position.

5. Set the first switches on for 10min, and then turn off the first switch, turn on the second switch, and then enter the room.

There are three possible scenarios

a. Bulb is on, therefore, the second switch is the correct one.

b. Bulb is off and on touching bulb, you will find bulb to be warm, therefore, the 1st switch is the correct one

c. Bulb is off and on touching second bulb, you will find bulb to be cool, therefore, the 3rd bulb is the correct one

6. Happy Birthday

7.He stood on a block of ice and waited for it to melt.

8. All you have to do is burn the first rope from both the ends and the second rope from one end only simultaneously. The first rope will burn in 30 minutes (half of an hour since we burned from both sides) while the other rope would have burnt half. At this moment, light the second rope from the other end as well. Where the second rope would have taken half an hour more to burn completely, it will take just 15 minutes as we have lit it from the other end too.

Thus you have successfully calculated 30+15 = 45 minutes with the help of the two given ropes.

9. Newspaper delivery man was the murderer because absence of Wednesday and Thursday newspapers. This indicates he already know there is no one to read it.

10. The man and the chicken cross the river. He leaves the chicken on the other side and goes back across. The man then takes the fox across the river and he brings the chicken back. This time he leaves the chicken and he takes the corn across and leaves it with the fox. He then returns to pick up the chicken and heads across the river one last time.

11. 17 minutes

The initial solution most people will think of is to use the fastest person as an usher to guide everyone across. How long would that take? 10 + 1 + 7 + 1 + 2 = 21 minutes but that is not the fastest time to cross.

To reduce the amount of time, we should find a way for 10 and 7 to cross together. If they cross together, then we need one of them to come back to get the others, which would be too slow. We need to have 1 waiting on the other side to bring the torch back. The fastest way to get 1 across and be back is to use 2 to usher 1 across. So let's put all this together.

1 and 2 go cross

2 comes back

7 and 10 go across

1 comes back

1 and 2 go across (done)

Total time = 2 + 2 + 10 + 1 + 2 = 17 minutes

12. Mark picks 4 marbles.

Explanation:

No matter how many marbles Vince picks, Mark needs to make sure that only 1 marble is left after his move, So that Vince needs to pick the last marble.

Example:

If Vince picks 1, Mark picks 5

If Vince picks 2, Mark picks 4

If Vince picks 5, Mark picks 1

13. Anybody will prefer the shop in the South End for sure. Since there are only two barbers in the town, the one running the shop in South End must have gotten his hair done by the one running the shop in the North End and vice versa. Thus, if the barber in the South End has a shabby haircut, it must be due to the incompetence of the North End barber.

14. You will have to ask, "I have a number in my mind that is either 2 or 3. Is the number that I have in my mind smaller or equal to the number that you are thinking of?"

If Shelly replies with no, he is thinking of the number 1.

If Shelly replies with yes, he is thinking of the number 3.

If Shelly replies with don't know, he is thinking of the number 2.

15. 25 Fruits

Remember we told you that Tanner is a witty trader. So his sole motive is to get rid of the sacks as fast as he can.

For the first sack:

He must be able to fill fruits from one sack to other two sacks. Assume that he is able to do that after X check points. Now to find X

(Space in first sack) X + (Space in second sack) X = (Remaining fruits in Third Sack) $30 - X$ X = 10 Thus after 10 checkpoints, Tanner will be left with only 2 sacks containing 30 fruits each.

Now he must get rid of the second sack.

For that, he must fill the fruits from second sack to the first sack. Assume that he manages to do that after Y checkpoints.

(Space in First Sack) Y = (Remaining fruits in second sack) $30 - Y$ Y = 15

Thus after he has crossed 25 checkpoints, he will be left be one sack with 30 fruits in it. He has to pass five more checkpoints where he will have to give five fruits and he will be left with twenty five fruits once he has crossed all thirty check points.

16. The woman started walking across the bridge when the guard was inside the hut. She walked all the time he was inside (5 minutes) and then turned and moved back towards the kingdom. On approaching the kingdom and since she "was an outsider," she was escorted out.

17. If the person killed themselves, they would not have been able to rewind the cassette. Thus it is clear someone else killed them.

18. They pile up the bricks and dirt from the tunnel to stand on.

19. Teal could only be wearing grey or red and we know that there is already someone else wearing the grey shirt so Mr. Teal could only be wearing the red shirt. Mr. Grey could have only been wearing a teal or a red shirt, and red is already taken, so Mr. Grey is wearing a teal shirt. Mr. Red, then, can be the only one wearing the grey shirt.

20. Two minutes (between 9:59 and 10:01)

21. Four. 3 placed flat on the table in a triangle (touching each other) and put the fourth one on top of them in the middle.

22. A grandfather, a father, and a son are the ones who went fishing. The Father and his father and the son and his son. 2 Fathers and 2 Sons but three people who catch three fish.

23. Once the water is boiling, start the three-minute timer and five-minute timer. When the three-minute timer runs out, put the egg in the boiling water. When the five-minute timer runs out, two minutes have elapsed and it is time take the egg out of the water.

24. Miss the first time on purpose. If you try to hit Frank and do, then Sally goes next and she will hit you for sure. If you aim at Sally and manage hit her then Frank will go for you.

If you miss on your first turn, Frank will go for Sally for sure because she has better aim. If he hits her then it's just you and Frank, but you go first. If he misses her then Sally will go for Frank and it will be just you and Sally, but, again, you are going first. This will give you the best odds of winning, even as the weakest player.

25. The wise son bought a candle and a box of matches. After lighting the candle, the light filled the entire room.

26. When she thought she was nearing the equator, Chandra filled the sink and allowed the water to drain away down the plughole. When the water reversed direction when going down the drain, she knew the ship had crossed the equator.

27. Take a coin from the chest labeled 50/50. If you pick a gold coin, you know that chest must contain all gold coins (it can't be the 50/50 chest because all the chests are incorrectly labeled). So, the chest labeled silver must be the 50/50 chest and the one labeled gold must be the silver chest.

114

On the other hand if you pick a silver coin, you know that chest must contain all silver coins, the one labeled silver must be the gold chest and the one labeled gold must be the 50/50 chest.

28. If the first prisoner had seen two red hats on the other two prisoners, he would have known that he was wearing a white hat as there were only two red hats to begin with. As he didn't know what color hat he had, this means the other two prisoners must either have been both wearing white hats or one wearing a white hat and the other a black one.

The second prisoner would know this once the first prisoner is unable to say what color his hat is, i.e. the second prisoner now knows that either both he and the blind prisoner are wearing white hats or one of them is wearing white and the other black. So if the blind prisoner was wearing a black hat, the second prisoner would know that he must be wearing a white hat.

As the second prisoner couldn't work out what color hat he was wearing, this told the blind prisoner that he must be wearing a white hat (if the blind prisoner was wearing a black hat, the second prisoner would have been able to deduce that he was wearing a white hat).

29. White. The only place you can walk 2 miles south, then east for 2 miles, then north for 2 miles and end up back at your starting point is the North Pole. Polar bears are the only bears that live at the North Pole, and they are white.

30. 2 men

31. Put it against the wall

32. Henry drinks the first very large glass, turns it over and places it over top the very small glass. Gwen cannot violate the rules to get to her glass and Henry drinks his second glass, winning the bet easily.

33. Parachutes

34. Son-1: 1 11 21 31 41 51 61 71 81

Son-2: 2 12 22 32 42 52 62 72 73

Son-3: 3 13 23 33 43 53 63 64 74

Son-4: 4 14 24 34 44 54 55 65 75

Son-5: 5 15 25 35 45 46 56 66 76

Son-6: 6 16 26 36 37 47 57 67 77

Son-7: 7 17 27 28 38 48 58 58 78

Son-8: 8 18 19 29 39 49 59 69 79

Son-9: 9 10 20 30 40 50 60 70 80

35. The code is 645

Explanation :

a) From Clues 1st and 2nd we know that one 7 is not in the code

b) From Clue 2nd we know that 7, 3, and 8 are not part of code

c) From Clue 3rd we know that 4 and 6 are part of code

d) From Clue 5th we know that 1 and 2 are not part of the code as we know 6 is part of the code and just 1 of 3 numbers is part of code.

e) From Clue 4th we know that 5 is also in the code as 8 and 1 are not part of code. So the code is: 645

36. A: The candies in the boxes will be as follows:

Box 1 = 1

Box 2 = 2

Box 3 = 4

Box 4 = 8

Box 5 = 16

Box 6 = 32

Box 7 = 64

Box 8 = 128

Box 9 = 256

We will place the number of candies left in box 10.

Box 10 = 489

If you try now, you will be able to do what is asked.

37. The intruder was immediately stabbed. Thus the knife was in the wife's hand. This implies that she was waiting to kill her husband, Inspector Hash.

38. On the first dice, you write 0, 1, 2, 3, 5, and 7

On the second dice, you can write 0, 1, 2, 4, 6, and 8.

You need 1 and 2 on both the dice to display 11 and 22. Also, we need 0 on both die to display dates from 01 to 09. Every number is accounted for except 06, 16, and 26. To get these numbers, simply flip the 9.

39. World War 1 was named for the existence of World War 2. World War I was not called WWI when it was fought. Thus it would not say World War 1 on the medal.

40. The man asked the king that he wanted to die of old age.

41. The size of the chocolate is 2 x 8 squares. Thus, you need to have 2 x 8 = 16 pieces. Every time you break the chocolate, you will get one extra piece.

Thus, to get 16 pieces, you must break it (16 - 1) = 15 times.

42. The children can get 19 sweets in for their wrappers. Out of 77 wrappers, 75 will be used to buy 15 sweets and two will be left spare. The 15 sweets will create 15 empty wrappers that can be exchanged to get three sweets. Three sweets will return three wrappers which will help them buy another candy when used with the two wrappers from earlier.

15 + 3 + 1 = 19

43. From 36 blocks there are 36 items made. The iron shavings are enough to make 6 blocks. Which make 6 more items. But don't stop here. The new shavings are good for 1 more item for a total of 43.

44. $35/70 + 148/296 = 1$

45. The baker who had three loaves should get one coin and the baker who had five loaves should get seven coins. If there were eight loaves and three men, each man ate two and two-thirds loaves. So the first baker gave the shepherd one-third of a loaf and the second baker gave the shepherd two and one-third loaves. Thus the baker who gave one-third of a loaf should get one coin and the one who gave seven-thirds of a loaf should get seven coins.

46. Fill the 5 oz. and 11 oz. Containers from the 24 oz. container. This leaves 8 oz. in the 24 oz. bottle. Next empty the 11 oz. bottle by pouring the contents in to the 13 oz. bottle. Fill the 13 oz. bottle from the 5 oz. container (with 2 oz.) and put the remaining 3 oz. in the 11 oz. bottle. This leaves the 5 oz. container empty. Now pour 5 oz. from the 13 oz. bottle in to the 5 oz. bottle leaving 8 oz. in the 13 oz. bottle. Finally, pour the 5 oz. bottle contents in to the 11 oz. bottle giving 8 oz. in this container.

47. The daughter should pick envelope 1. Statements 1 and 2 were false, and the only true statement was statement 3. If the check was in envelope 1, that would make statement 1 false, statement 2 false, and statement 3 is the only true statement. If the check was in

envelope 2, statements 1 and 2 would both be true. If the check was in envelope 3, statements 1 and 3 would both be true.

48. The black car was a hearse.

49. First he split them in to piles of 3, 3, and 2 blocks. Then he weighs both groups of 3 with each other. If they equal each other, then he knows the heavier cinder block is one of the 2 other blocks. He can then weigh them to find the heaver one. If the stacks of 3 blocks do not balance, he will weigh 2 of the 3 blocks from the heavier pile. If they balance he will know the brick left unweighed is heavier one. If they do not balance, he will know the heavier one.

50. One

51. Pour the milk from the 2nd cup to the 5th cup.

52. Five. There are only four different colors, so five socks you have at least two of the same color.

53. No, the statement is false.

54. The poison was frozen in the ice.

55. She tells them that she will hand out the detention to the student who skips the quiz whose name comes first alphabetically. This student won't skip because they know they are getting a detention if they do. The next person alphabetically will then know that they will get a detention so they won't skip either, and so on. Therefore all students will take the quiz.

56. Yes, from the information you know 1 is honest and 99 are liars.

One of them is honest, making the first fact true. Then if you take the honest man and any other politician, the other politician must be a liar to satisfy the second piece of information, 'If you take any two politicians, at least one of them is a liar.' So the other 99 are liars.

57. Touch the end of one bar (bar A) to the middle of the other bar (bar B) forming a 'T' shape. If the bars are attracted then bar A is magnetized and if they are not attracted then bar B is the magnet. This is because magnets have fields at the poles but not in the middle. So the end would attract and middle would not.

58. 4 bees and 3 flowers

59. Make a pile of 10 coins and a pile of 90 coins, flip all of the coins in the pile of 10 and it is guaranteed that the piles have the same number of tails no matter what the make up of the original pile was.

60. The mail guy did it because if he checked between page numbers 1 and 2 page numbers 2 and 3 are opposite sides of one page and could not hold the dollar bill

61. He pushed the cork down in to the bottle and shook out the coin.

62. 2 years, the house won't go up at all because trees grow from the top, not the bottom.

63. 20 times. (8, 18, 28, 38, 48, 58, 68, 78, 80, 81, 82, 83, 84, 85, 86, 87, 88, 89, 98).

64. He can cut a one pound slab off and a two pound slab off. This would leave a one pound, two pound, and three pound block. On the first day he leaves the one pound block. On the second day he leaves the two pound block. On the third day he leaves the three pound block. On the fourth day he leaves the three pound and one pound blocks. On the fifth day he leaves the three pound and two pound blocks. On the last day he leaves all of them.

65. To do this you just have to get another BTZ and cut all four pills in half taking a half from each pill. Do the same the next day and you will definitely get the right amount of each pill for the two days.

66. He just copies the great chess computer moves exactly on both boards, going first on one and second on the other. He waits for the great player to make his first move on the first board and copies this on the board he goes first on. He then waits for the chess player to make his move on that board and copies it on the other board. He alternates moves on the two boards like this until the game is over and he ties on both or wins one and loses one.

67. He is celebrating in the southern hemisphere

68. First she has to draw one of the papers and destroy it somehow. Then they will check the box and see that the other paper says 'YES.' so they know that she drew the paper that said 'NO.' In this case, she doesn't have to marry the king.

69. They realized that it would take 5 people to execute this plan. There is one in every corner and one moving from one corner to another at all times. So somebody was already in the cabin.

70. First you divide the 25 horses into 5 groups of 5. You conduct the 5 races and take all of the fastest horses in those races and have a race with them, giving you the fastest horse. Then you take the remaining 24 horses (excluding the fastest) and remove the 4th and 5th horses in the first set of 5 races (since they definitely have 3 horses faster than them), leaving you with 14 horses. Next you can remove all of the horses that were beat in the preliminary race by the horses that got 4th and 5th in the championship race, leaving you with 8 horses. Finally, you can remove the horses that remain that lost to the 3rd place horse in the final race in the preliminary race and the horse that got 3rd in the preliminary to the horse that got 2nd in the championship race, leaving you with 5 horses.

You can then run a final race where the 1st and 2nd place horses are the 2nd and 3rd fastest. Then you know the 3 fastest horses. So it would take 7 races.

Chapter Five: Four Stars Riddle

1. A candle

2. Music

3. A deciduous tree

4. A thorn

5. A needle and thread

6. Words

7. A doorbell

8. Electricity

9. A pencil

10. A train

11. Glasses

12. Space

13. A window

14. Bread

15. Sunglasses

16. A bar of soap

17. A library

18. The Moon

19. Blood

20. A river

21. A stage

22. A smile

23. A snake

24. Poison

25. A thimble

26. A snowman

27. An alibi

28. The gems in order are: Amethyst, Emerald, Ruby, Pearl, Diamond, Tiger's eye, Cubic Zirconium, Opal.

29. An ax

30. A bullet

31. Trust

32. Beauty

33. They are fish and their tank was broken. They were placed in the bowl of water.

34. Arrows.

35. Your back

36. Knowledge

37. A prank

38. Chain

39. A record

40. A mouse in a live trap

41. A cherry

42. Family tree

43. Fireworks

44. A castle

45. A ring

46. Sand

47. Chalk

48. Water

49. Fur

Chapter Six: Five Stars Riddle

1. A heart

2. DAVID (Roman Numerals play a key part of this answer)

3. The hands of a clock (Hour hand, minute hand, second hand)

4. A splinter

5. A mailbox

6. A beehive

7. A book

8. A flower

9. A film negative

10. Paper

11. A diamond

12. A violin

13. An egg

14. A lie

15. A broom

16. A doll

17. A snail

18. A puzzle

19. The Moon

20. Ego

21. A grudge

22. Risks

23. Balance

24. Memory

25. A computer

26. A cave

27. Winter

28. A deal

29. A legend or fable

30. Hunger

31. Ice

32. Rust

33. Thunder and lightning

34. Dust

35. Thoughts

36. A watch

Chapter Seven: Six Stars Riddle

1. Mercury

2. A bell

3. A bank

4. A cat

5. Blame

6. Fear

7. An eye

8. Courage

9. Justice

10. A bookmark

11. A riddle

12. A pupil

13. Purpose

14. A feather

15. Punishment

16. Twins

17. Redemption